W9-CDM-593

CONTENTS

HOW ANIMALS COMMUNICATE

REBECCA STEFOFF

Cavendish
Square

New York

This book is dedicated to CALVIN RAY JAGUAR BLACKHEART.

With special thanks to Dr. Michael D. Breed of the Environmental, Population, and Organismic Biology department at the University of Colorado, Boulder, for reviewing the text of this book.

Published in 2014 by Cavendish Square Publishing, LLC
303 Park Avenue South, Suite 1247, New York, NY 10010

Library of Congress Cataloging-in-Publication Data
Stefoff, Rebecca, [date]-
How animals communicate / Rebecca Stefoff. • p. cm.—(Animal behavior revealed)
Includes bibliographical references and index.
ISBN 978-1-60870-510-8 (hardcover) • ISBN 978-1-62712-021-0 (paperback) • ISBN 978-1-60870-612-9 (ebook)
1. Animal communication—Juvenile literature. I. Title.
QL776.S74 2012 • 591.59—dc22 • 2010036706

Art Director: Anahid Hamparian • Series Designer: Alicia Mikles

Photo research by Laurie Platt Winfrey, Carousel Research, Inc.

The photographs in this book are used by permission and through the courtesy of:
Cover: Alamy / Juniors Bildarchiv; Alamy: Blickwinkel, 25; Manfred Grebler, 27; Afripics.com, 36; Steve Bloom Images, 42; Stu Porter, 49; Jose Ruiz/Nature Picture Library, 55. Corbis: E.&P. Bauer/Zofa, 67. Getty Images: Martin Harvey/Gallo Images, 4; Nina Leen/ Time & Life Pictures, 7; Cyril Ruoso/JH Editorial/ Minden Pictures, 22; Photolibrary, 26; Konrad Wothe/ Minden Pictures, 29; Gary Bell/ Taxi, 38. Minden Pictures: John Downer, 17; Norbert Wu, 18; Tui de Roy, 43; Georgette Douwma/ NPL,47 ; Ahup Shah, 60; Jane Burton, 64; Mark Moffett, 72. National Geographic Images: Jason Edward, 15; Norbert Rosing, 33. Newscom: 131/Zuma Press, 13. Photo Researchers: Dr. Merlin Tuttle/ Bat Conservation International, 21; Sinclair Stammers, 31; Robert Noonan, 65; Lena Untidt/ Bonnier Publications, 70. Superstock: Robert Harding Picture Library, 10, 45; Tier und Naturfotografie, 41; Superstock, 58.

Printed in the United States of America

INVESTIGATING ANIMAL BEHAVIOR

Why would scientists build a robot bee, dig through piles of rhinoceros dung, or make recordings of hyenas giggling? To explore the world of animal communication.

New discoveries are changing our view of how animals communicate with each other. Experts have learned that certain monkeys have grammar, squids use a secret language, and male and female beetles read each other's messages through their feet. Communication takes place throughout the animal kingdom in a wide variety of ways. By learning more about how animals talk to each other, scientists are gaining a better understanding of the creatures that share the world with human beings.

People have always been fascinated by animals. Tens of thousands of years ago, our ancestors painted lifelike pictures of bears, bison, and deer on cave walls. Twenty-five centuries ago, Greek thinkers wrote about animals and their habits. Those writings were the beginning of **zoology**, the scientific study of animals.

The giggling, whooping calls of spotted hyenas sound like human laughter. Legends used to say that hyenas laughed to lure people into becoming their prey. Now scientists know that the sounds are the hyenas' complex communication system.

5

In time zoologists wondered why animals do the things they do. When a baby monkey shows a fear of snakes, is the fear an **instinct**— a built-in pattern of behavior that is programmed into the monkey's genes? Or has the baby learned to be afraid because its mother and the other monkeys in its troop scream and run when they see a snake? Did those monkeys communicate their fear of snakes to the baby? Questions like these gave rise to **ethology**, the branch of zoology that studies animal behavior.

Ethology became established as a science in the twentieth century. One of its pioneers was an Austrian zoologist named Konrad Lorenz, who studied the behavior of geese and ducks. When these birds hatch, they usually see their mother right away, and afterward they follow her around. Lorenz wondered what would happen if young birds hatched apart from others of their **species**. He experimented with geese and found that newly hatched birds bonded with the first thing they saw. Young geese that bonded with Lorenz followed him around as if he were their mother. Lorenz called this behavior imprinting.

Lorenz published his findings in 1935. The next year he met Niko-laas Tinbergen, a Dutch zoologist who was also curious about how animals react to signals from their environment. Together Tinbergen and Lorenz studied seagulls and ducks. They discovered that young birds raised by humans showed no fear of round or square cardboard cutouts, but they instinctively recognized shapes that signaled danger. When cutouts shaped like hawks and eagles were flown over their nests the birds became afraid, even though they had never seen those **predators**.

Konrad Lorenz's lifelong interest in wild geese grew from a book about these birds that he read as a child. In this photograph from 1964, he swims with graylag geese. The geese imprinted on him as soon as they hatched.

The work of Lorenz and Tinbergen was a step toward understanding animal instincts. In 1973 the two men, along with Karl von Frisch, an Austrian zoologist who studied bee behavior, shared the Nobel Prize, one of the highest scientific honors, for their work in the new science of ethology.

Tinbergen came up with four key questions to ask about the things that animals do. Today ethologists and animal behavior researchers still use those questions to guide their investigations. The questions are:

- What causes the animal's behavior? Scientists studying communication in chimpanzees, for example, might ask whether a certain cry or call is connected with playing, finding food, or fighting.
- Does the behavior change over the animal's lifetime? Are young chimpanzees' calls different from adults' calls? Do chimpanzees make more sounds as they grow older, or fewer?
- How does the animal's behavior compare with the way similar species behave? Are chimpanzee calls different from the sounds made by other great apes, such as gorillas?
- Does the behavior help or hurt the animal's chances of surviving and reproducing? Imagine that a chimpanzee spots a leopard and calls out in alarm. Does the sound draw other chimpanzees, confusing the predator with many possible targets? Or does the sound focus the leopard's attention on the first chimpanzee?

Tinbergen also warned other scientists against **anthropomorphism**, which is a fancy way of saying, "giving human qualities to animals." When we describe animals in human terms, such as saying, "Oh, that bear looks sad," we are anthropomorphizing. For a long time, anthropomorphism was strictly forbidden in ethology. In recent years, though, scientists have learned much about the inner lives of animals—how they think, feel, communicate, and play. Thinking that animals are completely different from people may be as big a mistake as thinking that they are just like people.

The study of animal behavior takes many forms. Some researchers, for example, focus on **psychology**, the study of human and animal minds, or on **evolution**, the study of how life on earth has developed and changed over time. **Sociobiologists** study animals that live in social groups, such as ants and prairie dogs. Behavioral ecologists look at how animals interact with their environments. Other researchers investigate animal intelligence and emotion.

This book explores how and why animals communicate with each other. Thousands of species of animals, not just those mentioned in this book, are sending and receiving messages right now. Scientists discover new and unexpected kinds of animal communication all the time—and more secrets are waiting to be discovered.

1. WHAT ARE ANIMALS "SAYING"?

Undercover watchers staked out a stretch of sandy coastline on the Arabian Sea. Day after day, hidden from view, they aimed cameras and microphones at the beach. The lurkers were not detectives or spies. They were biologists, and they were looking for ghosts.

The ghosts were actually crabs—pale-colored animals called ghost crabs that live on sandy shores in many parts of the world. The biologists were studying and recording the curious rituals of these crabs.

During the crabs' mating season, male crabs dug spiral burrows into the sand. The males then crouched at the burrow entrances while other crabs wandered along the beach. At times a crouching crab struck, or rapped, the sand repeatedly with one of its large front claws. This movement made a sound and sent vibrations through the ground.

Whenever a wandering crab approached a burrow, the burrow's owner, straightening his legs, raised himself to his full height. He then waved his claws and scuttled rapidly in a straight line or in circles, as if

Ghost crabs skitter through the surf. These hard-shelled creatures send messages to each other by beating their claws on the sand, sending rapping sounds across the beach.

dancing. If the wanderer came closer, the "dancer" moved farther from his burrow. Sometimes the dancer circled around and around the wanderer. After the wanderer moved away, the dancer returned to his burrow entrance. There he crouched and rapped again. This time he might hit both claws against the sand, as if a drummer were beating a drum.

Why did the male crabs rap, dance, and drum? They may have been trying to attract a wandering female or to scare off wandering males who might steal their burrow. The scientists could not tell from a distance whether the wanderers were male or female (picking them up for study would have disturbed the crabs' behavior). Now that scientists have the behavior recorded, future researchers may solve the mystery by examining the wandering crabs more closely. But the hidden watchers knew one thing—when the crabs rapped, drummed, and danced, they were communicating.

Message, Meaning, and Signal

"Animal communication" may bring to mind the chirping of birds or the howling of wolves. Communication between animals, though, takes many forms. Scientists define it in terms of behavior. Communication happens whenever an animal does something that is meant to change how another animal behaves.

A male firefly's blinking light, for example, flashes a courtship message: "I'm a male, and I'm looking for a female." The female firefly answers with her own signal: "I'm a female. Let's get together."

Earthworms communicate, too. Worms feel slimy because they produce mucus that helps them slither through the ground. When

Under attack by a robin, an earthworm floods the soil around it with alarm chemicals that will make any other earthworms in the area crawl away from danger.

an earthworm is startled or under attack, a special "alarm" chemical floods into its mucus. Other earthworms in the area sense this chemical through the soil and crawl away from danger.

Every communication has three parts: message, meaning, and signal. The message is what an animal sends. The meaning is how another animal interprets it. The signal is the form of the communication. Picture a robin yanking an earthworm out of the ground. The worm sends the message "Trouble!" The meaning to a nearby worm is "Get out of here!" The signal is the alarm chemical in the first worm's mucus.

Why Animals Communicate

Animals send and receive signals all the time. Most often they communicate with other animals of their own species. Sometimes, though, animals send messages to members of other species. It all depends on the reason for communicating.

Courtship. Communications aimed at attracting a mate or strengthening the bond between mates are courtship messages. The firefly's blinking light is one example. Another is the dance of the sage grouse, a bird found in the high deserts of the American West. Every spring, male sage grouse gather at special sites, called leks, where they strut and fan their tail feathers for hours to draw the attention of females.

Food. Some animals tell others in their family or social group about a food source they have found. In the 1980s scientists discovered that ravens—large black birds related to crows—give special calls known as yells when they find a dead animal. Raven yells passed from one bird to another can draw ravens to a moose or deer carcass from 30 miles (48 kilometers) away.

Territory. Animals send messages to protect or defend either their territory, mate, young, or food. During the mating season, small male songbirds called willow warblers choose a territory that contains insects to eat and a place to build a nest. Each bird sings to tell other males, "This territory is taken." If another male ignores the song and enters his territory, the first bird flaps his wings to shoo the intruder away.

Aggression. Scientists use the term *agonistic* to describe messages related to conflict, aggression, and power. Warnings and threats, such as a dog's growl or a bull's pawing at the ground, are **agonistic** communications. Messages that say an animal wants to avoid conflict—such as a dog crouching on the ground and wagging its tail—are agonistic communications, too. The term includes both sides of a conflict or possible conflict: the dominant, or stronger, animal and the submissive, or weaker, one.

Alarm. An animal that spots a predator may send an alarm message so that others in its group can run, hide, or bunch together against the predator. Among meerkats, small burrow-dwelling mammals of South Africa, a lookout keeps watch while others **forage** for food. At the sight of an eagle or a wild dog, the lookout shrieks an alarm call that sends all the meerkats dashing for their burrows.

Two meerkats keep watch while the rest of their clan dig in the sand for insects, scorpions, and other prey. The animals take turns at lookout duty, usually for about an hour each time. Lookouts stand up often to scan the sky and landscape for threats.

Bonding. Some behavior, such as grooming in lions and kissing in chimpanzees, builds bonds between animals that live in family or social groups. Often when two related female elephants meet, they bond by touching their trunks together or twining them around each other. This gesture may mean "Hello" or "I recognize you."

Prey to Predator. **Prey** animals sometimes send messages to discourage predators. When a springbok, a southern African antelope, catches sight of a lion or a leopard, it responds by stotting. This behavior—leaping high into the air—sends the message that the springbok is strong and nimble and would be hard to catch.

Liars and Eavesdroppers

Communication among humans is not always straightforward. People sometimes say things that are not true or listen in on conversations they are not meant to hear. This same behavior has been observed in the animal world, too.

When a fox gets close to a bird's nest, the bird may leave the nest and move to the ground. Instinctively, the bird will drag one wing as though it is injured and cannot fly. The fox is fooled into thinking that it will be easy prey. When the bird has lured the fox far enough from its nest, it flies away. Animal behavior scientists call this kind of behavior deceptive communication.

Lured to Death

Deceptive communication is a way of life for some creatures. Fireflies (winged beetles active at night) are common in many parts of

GETTING WILD

One way to learn about animal communication is to study tame animals or captive animals in zoos and wildlife parks. Another is to focus on easily trained species, such as mice and dogs, in laboratory experiments. Some **primatologists**—biologists who study apes and monkeys—study ape intelligence by seeing whether apes can "speak" to humans using sign language. To learn how animals communicate among themselves without human interference, however, scientists must observe them in their natural state—the wild.

Watching wildlife can be a challenge. Researchers have slogged through mosquito-infested swamps to record alligator calls and climbed the Himalayas to measure snow leopard paw prints. In her study of wild chimpanzees in Africa, the British primatologist Jane Goodall spent years just letting them get used to seeing her, first at a distance and then closer. In time the chimpanzees accepted Goodall as part of the landscape, and she was able to watch them going about their daily lives.

Just as **NASA** (National Aeronautics and Space Administration) sends robot probes into space to explore other worlds, biologists now use machines to explore animal behavior on Earth. To study white-tailed deer in North American forests, scientists captured deer, attached tiny cameras to their antlers, and released them. The "antler cams" revealed that deer communicate more through touching, nibbling each other, and grooming than anyone had suspected.

A camera mounted on a small remote-controlled truck lets wildlife researchers get close to lions.

The deep-sea anglerfish sends false messages to other fish using the spine on its fore-head, which ends in a glowing blob. The anglerfish twitches the spine like a fishing pole, with the blob as bait. When the small fish on the right approaches the bait, the anglerfish will swallow it. (The fish are lit in this photograph, but normally only the bait would be visible. It glows because of a chemical reaction called bioluminescence, which many sea creatures share.)

the world. Two or more similar species may live in the same area, but fireflies mate only with their own species. Many firefly species have organs in their abdomen that produce light through chemical reactions. In these species, males and females flash their lights to identify each other. Each species has its own male and female flash patterns.

Some female fireflies use trickery on the males of other species to get a meal. The females can imitate other species' signals. When the female sees flashing lights from a male of another species, she flashes back the "correct" female courting signal—but it's a trap. When the male flies over to mate with her, she eats him instead.

Overheard

Animals "eavesdrop" on messages that are not directed at them. For example, in 2002 scientists learned that some male songbirds listen in on fights between other males. It works this way: Birds A and B, squabbling over a tasty worm, make aggressive calls at each other. Bird A wins and gets the worm. Bird B gives up and goes away. Meanwhile, bird C builds a nest nearby.

Then one of the first two birds tries to move into C's territory. If the intruder is the bird that won the fight over the worm, C sings a long, loud territorial song to warn that bird to stay away. If the intruder is the bird that lost the fight, C's song is shorter and quieter because C, who overheard the fight, knows which bird is the bigger threat.

In cross-species communication an animal overhears and uses a message sent by an animal of a different species. When a hawk soars over a backyard birdfeeder, a sharp-eyed blue jay may sound an alarm call to tell other jays to hide under bushes or in tree branches. The jay is communicating with other jays in the area, some of which may be its offspring, but red squirrels recognize the jay's message and run for cover, too.

Scientists are still in the early stages of studying cross-species communication, but already they know that several species "listen in" on each other's alarm calls. Vervet monkeys in Africa recognize the alarm calls of birds called superb starlings. The alarm calls of another **primate** species, Diana monkeys, are understood by another kind of bird, the yellow-casqued hornbill. The animal world may be filled with messages that cross species lines.

Eavesdroppers can be deadly, as tungara frogs know. These frogs live in the Central American country of Panama. Males gather at night and make sounds to attract mates. Sometimes, though, their calls are received by fringe-lipped bats—which eat frogs. The bats follow the sound of the frogs' calls, and if the frogs do not stop calling in time, the bats snatch up a tasty meal.

All of the Senses

The variety of animal communications is vast. Every sense that humans have—and some senses that humans do not have—play a part in animal communication. Members of the animal kingdom communicate using the five senses of smell, taste, sight, sound, and touch, and also through vibrations and even electricity.

The ghost crabs on the beach sent messages to three senses: sight, sound, and vibration. Other crabs saw the dancing, heard the rapping and drumming, and felt the rapping and drumming through the ground.

A bat swoops down on a tungara frog. The frog had been calling to other frogs, but unfortunately its messages were heard by a winged predator.

Komodo dragons, the world's largest lizards, feed on the carcasses of dead animals, which they can smell from miles away. Flicking its tongue helps the lizard sense odor chemicals carried by the air. Earth, water, and air are full of information, but human senses are unaware of much of it.

Human senses cannot receive many of the messages that animals send to each other. That may be a good thing—after all, who wants to smell or taste an earthworm's alarm mucus? Science has shown that humans are surrounded by animal communications. Although we will probably never know exactly what a bird's cry means to another bird, there are still many more hidden messages to be uncovered.

2. SPEAKING WITH SMELLS

From fresh cinnamon rolls to garbage dumpsters, the world is full of smells—good and bad. Humans smell only a fraction of the odors around them, but many animals have a powerful sense of smell. They can receive chemical messages sent by other animals. Scientists recently discovered that even the lowly cockroach uses its sense of smell to organize cockroach communities.

The Sense of Smell

All animals, including humans, smell and taste things because of special cells called **chemoreceptors**. There are two kinds of chemoreceptors. **Gustatory** receptors, which are connected to the sense of taste, react to things they touch. **Olfactory** receptors are connected to the sense of smell. As these receptors pick up odors carried in air or water, scent communication travels from one animal to another.

Smells are caused by **molecules** that act as chemical signals. When those molecules come into contact with an animal's olfactory receptors, the receptors send a message to the animal's brain or nervous system, triggering the sensation of smell. The number of chemo-receptors varies from species to species. The skin inside the human nose has about 5 million olfactory receptors. A dog's nose has 220 million and so can smell things that a human's cannot.

Noses and mouths contain chemoreceptors, but these cells can be located in other places, too. Many insects have chemoreceptors on their antennae or on fine, small hairs scattered across their body. An earthworm's whole body is covered with chemoreceptors that pick up signals from the air, water, and soil.

Pheromone Power

A **pheromone** is a chemical given off by an animal for communication. Depending upon the species, an animal can release pheromones in its breath, in its urine or feces, through the pores of its skin, or from special scent glands. Also depending on the species, scent glands may be located on the animal's forehead, cheeks, feet, belly, or legs.

Weasels, deer, and cats are just a few of the animals that have scent glands on the backside, near the anus. A cat also has scent glands on the sides of the face. When a cat rubs its cheek against a door frame or its human's leg, it is leaving a scent mark that other cats can smell.

Pheromones cause other animals of the same species to react. Some pheromones, called primers, bring about a physical response. One example is found in ordinary house mice. A male mouse's urine contains a primer pheromone. When a pregnant female mouse smells it, her body automatically aborts her unborn young if their father was

This tender moment is a form of feline communication. By rubbing the scent gland in its cheek against a person's leg, the cat is leaving a mark that other cats can smell. Scent-rubbing is one of cats' instinctive ways of marking their territory and bonding with each other.

Feet are for tasting as well as walking, if you're a fly. The fine hairs on a fly's foot contain organs that perceive tastes such as sweet and bitter. The insect samples its food by walking on it.

any mouse other than the one who sprayed the urine. Afterward she is ready to mate with the male that left the primer pheromone. The primer pheromone gives a male more opportunities to mate and father his own young.

Pheromones that directly affect behavior are called releasers. They trigger certain actions instead of physical changes. When a female tiger is ready to mate, for example, her urine contains a releaser pheromone that male tigers can smell. A male that senses this pheromone will follow the scent to the female.

CURL THAT LIP!

Have you ever seen a horse curl its upper lip, showing its teeth in a strange open-mouthed grin? The horse was doing something that scientists call the flehmen response. (The name comes from the German word meaning "to curl the lip.") The flehmen response pulls air across the roof of the horse's mouth. A patch of tissue there is especially sensitive to pheromones in the air. Scientists call this sense organ the **vomeronasal organ** (also called Jacobson's organ).

Giraffes, goats, cows, elephants, pigs, and zebras have vomeronasal organs. So do cats, including tigers and lions. Most lizards and all snakes have them—when a lizard or snake flicks its tongue, it is drawing air onto its vomeronasal organ. Some monkeys have vomeronasal organs, but scientists disagree about whether the organ is present in humans.

A horse that seems to be laughing or grimacing is really drawing air toward a special sense organ in the roof of its mouth. Other animals share this behavior, called the flehmen response.

Each species' releaser pheromones are unique to that species. Pheromones were probably among the first signals used to send messages between animals, and they are still many animals' main form of chemical communication.

What about Taste?

Smell plays a huge role in animal communication, but what about taste? Animals use the sense of taste mostly to test possible food sources. Flies have gustatory chemoreceptors on their feet. They taste sugar, salt, and water through their feet.

Taste sometimes plays a small role in communication. When a male tiger smells a female's scent mark, for example, he may also taste the mark with his tongue, possibly double-checking the meaning of the signal.

Releaser Pheromones in Action

Animals communicate with pheromones for various reasons. Sex pheromones signal that an animal is ready to mate. Marker pheromones send messages such as "I've been here" or "This is my territory." Alarm pheromones warn others of danger.

Recruitment pheromones call animals together. Swarming behavior is triggered by these chemicals. Worker bees can release a pheromone that causes all the bees in the swarm to cluster together. A pheromone given off only by the queen bee makes the workers form a buzzing cluster around her.

Worker and queen bees can release pheromones that summon other bees to cluster together in a swarm for traveling to a new hive location or fighting an attacker.

Pheromones also serve as individual "identity badges." They help animals recognize each other. Sometimes pheromones signal each animal's rank in the social group.

Some pheromones travel quickly but don't last long. Alarm pheromones are a good example. To be useful, a signal such as the earthworm's "I'm being attacked!" must reach nearby worms fast, but it is needed for only a few moments. Alarm pheromones dissolve soon so that they don't clutter up the environment with "out of date" messages. Pheromones that mark an animal's territory are different. These chemicals may have to last a long time—sometimes even for months—when the animal has a large territory to patrol.

Insects: Top Chemical Communicators

Chemical communication is highly developed among insects, especially those that live in social groups, such as ants. If a fire ant foraging away from its nest finds a dead beetle that is too big for it to carry, the ant returns to its nest. Along the way the ant lays a scent trail from a gland on the underside of its abdomen.

The ant's trail is made of recruitment pheromones, the kind that tells other ants to gather. Once the first ant reaches the nest, it returns along the trail to the dead beetle. This time, other ants, drawn by the pheromones, follow it. When enough ants reach the beetle, they drag or carry it back to the nest.

Sometimes an insect's own pheromones are not good enough to get the job done. A male orchid bee collects scented oils and chemicals from flowers, fruit, rotting wood, fungi, and tree sap. He stores

When an ant finds a dead beetle that is too heavy to carry, it leaves a pheromone trail that allows it, and other ants, to return, find the beetle, and bring it back to their ant nest and eat it.

them in pouches on his hind legs, where they blend into a complex scent. At courtship time, the bee moves his stash of perfume to the base of his wings. When he flies around a female bee, his wings blow the scent to her. The perfume made by the male bee acts like a phero-mone and sends the mating message.

In 2006 scientists reported that cockroaches use scent to make group decisions. In a study of how cockroaches share living space, fifty roaches were given a choice of three shelters, each large enough to hold more than fifty bugs. All fifty roaches moved into one shelter, and the other two were left empty. When the fifty roaches were given shelters that could hold only forty bugs each, they did not form one group of forty and another group of ten. Instead, they formed two groups of twenty-five.

Why did the cockroaches make these decisions? Scientists cannot yet answer that question, but they know *how* the bugs communicate. Although roaches can see each other, they rely heavily on scent receptors in their antennae. Each time the experimenters put the cockroaches into a container with a new arrangement of shelters, the roaches spent a long time touching each other with their antennae before dividing themselves up and entering the shelters. The insects may be able to count how many are in their group.

Reptiles: Adaptable Iguanas and Sneaky Snakes

The desert iguana is a reptile that lives in the hot, dry American Southwest. It marks its territory with scent from glands on the undersides of its hind legs—but the scent chemicals burn off quickly in the fierce desert heat. Luckily, the desert iguana is well adapted to life in its harsh environment.

In addition to odor molecules, the secretions from the iguana's glands contain molecules that reflect ultraviolet light, a kind that is invisible to humans but visible to iguanas. This light turns the secretions into visual signals. The iguanas see each other's territorial markings even after the scent has faded.

Like any other form of communication, scent can be used for trickery. Take the case of the red-sided garter snake, found across much of North America. These snakes hibernate during the winter. In the spring they wake up ready to mate. The female gives off a pheromone that attracts males—lots of males. A hundred or more of them may slither to her side. Only one male snake from this squirming mass, called a mating ball, will get to mate with her, so the competition is fierce.

Following the pheromone trail of a female red-sided garter snake, male snakes have formed a writhing mating ball, competing for a chance to mate with the female.

To get ahead in the mating contest, some male red-sided garter snakes use deception. The male can produce a little of the female sex pheromone. When the attention of the other male snakes is drawn to *his* female smell and away from the *real* female, it leads to less competition for this deceitful male. The trick works. More than two-thirds of the male snakes that succeed in mating use the decoy female pheromone.

Mammals: Spray (or Spread) It to Say It

Brown hyenas live in clans of up to a dozen or so individuals on the African plains. The clan shares a den, but each individual looks for food alone. Foraging takes place in the clan's home range, which covers 90 to 185 square miles (235–480 square kilometers). The largest ranges are about the size of the city of Los Angeles—a lot of ground for a dozen animals to cover.

To communicate with clan members as well as strangers, a hyena uses a type of marking called pasting. By raising its tail and rubbing its backside against grass stems or shrubs, the animal deposits two secretions from a pouch near the anus. One secretion is white and waxy and lasts for a month or more. The other, black and watery, starts to fade after a few hours. Scientists think that the white, long-lasting secretion is a territorial marker that tells strange hyenas that the range is occupied. The black, short-lived secretion tells hyenas in the clan which of their fellow clan members passed by recently.

Hyenas' communication networks need constant maintenance. When a hyena is out foraging, it stops to paste half a dozen times within a single square mile. At any moment, twenty thousand pastings may be releasing pheromones across a clan's range.

Black and white rhinoceroses are native to Africa, too. These big mammals create gigantic chemical signals that grow into community message boards.

A dominant, or top-ranking, male rhino has lots of ways to say "This is my territory." He pauses often to mark a spot with his scent by rubbing his horn against the ground or a tree or bush. Afterward he scrapes the ground with each foot in turn; this activity leaves more scent marks (and also the visual message of the torn earth). To make sure no one misses the message, he also urinates on the spot. Several times.

The male rhino has yet another way to announce his ownership of the territory. He deposits his dung, or feces, in the same places time after time. He kicks some of the dung afterward to get it on his feet so that he can then spread it across his territory as he walks. The rhino's territory may contain twenty or thirty of these big dunghills, which scientists call middens—basically, big piles of poo.

Black rhino middens may cover up to 32 square yards (26.8 square meters). That's about eight times the size of a king-sized bed, although most middens are smaller. Once a dominant male establishes a midden, other rhinos living in the territory also use it. Female and young rhinos, as well as lower-ranking males, make their own dung deposits at the middens, but without the kicking. From the pheromones in a rhino's dung, other rhinos can tell whether the animal was male or female and, if female, ready for mating or pregnant.

A bull rhinoceros kicks his midden, or dunghill, spreading freshly deposited waste that contains pheromones that declare his identity. When the rhino leaves to patrol his territory, dung from his feet will leave his calling card far and wide.

Sea otters also mark their territory with piles of feces, called spraints. Spraints communicate something else as well: they act as signposts pointing the way to fresh water. Sea otters swim and hunt in salt water but must come ashore to drink fresh water. In places where fresh water can be hard to find, such as the rocky islands of the North Sea, generations of sea otters have built up trails of spraints that lead from the shore to the water sources. The spraint trails are like public service announcements, helping any and all otters find a place to drink. River otters also communicate with spraints, leaving piles to mark their territories.

Scent can communicate kinship as well as territorial claims. Many mammals that live in social groups, such as lions and mongooses, rub their scent gland secretions onto each other. This behavior is a way of saying, "We're all part of the pack." Scent helps young animals learn to recognize their relatives and the other individuals in the group.

Smell Works Well—Sometimes

Communicating by smell has some advantages. Unlike vision, the sense of smell works just as well by night as by day. Smells can travel over great distances and around obstacles. Male and female moths can catch each other's pheromones across distances of up to 6 miles (9.6 km), if the wind is in their favor.

Scent-based messages also have staying power. Some pheromones continue to broadcast their message to a wide audience for weeks or even months. At times, though, animals need to send instant messages. For quick communication, sight and sound are ideal.

3. SIGHT AND SOUND

Nearly all creatures send visual messages, and most also communicate with sounds. Birds, dolphins, and primates make many different calls, and scientists have recently discovered that hyenas use sound in ways that no one suspected.

Sight and sound messages can backfire by calling attention to the sender. If a predator sees a flash of bright color or hears a call, the sender of the message may end up as dinner. Still, sight and sound are good for fast communication.

Appearance Matters

An animal's appearance is a kind of sight-based communication. Animals recognize others of their own species by the way they look. Sometimes an animal's colors or markings send a message to other species as well.

Australia's blue-ringed octopus is notorious for being the most venomous octopus on the planet. The animal's bright blue rings are a form of communication—visual warning signs that discourage predators from attacking the toxic creature.

Warning Signs

The blue-ringed octopus and the poison arrow frog are highly venomous. Their bright colors and dramatic patterns also make them highly visible. Scientists think that these colors and patterns warn predators that the animals are toxic. An arrow frog's shiny blue-and-yellow skin is saying, "Don't mess with me. I'm poisonous. I'll make you sick or maybe kill you."

An animal that is not poisonous may look like a poisonous animal. The coral snake, which has a toxic bite, is black with bright yellow and red stripes. Several harmless snakes, including milk snakes and king snakes, look similar to the venomous coral snake. The look-alike's appearance fools predators.

Quick Changes

Some animals can change their appearance instantly. Fireflies flash lights, frilled lizards fan the flaps of skin around their neck, and cockatoos raise the crest of long feathers on top of their head.

Color change is a fast form of communication for certain fish and lizards. Chameleons are a group of lizards famous for their rapid transformations. In less than a minute a chameleon can turn from camouflage green, a color that blends into the background of leaves, to red with white stripes, a pattern that warns other chameleons to keep away. If another chameleon ignores the message and there is a fight, the loser may turn brown to send the message "I give up."

These instant color changes are possible because the animals have cells called **chromatophores** in their skin. Chromatophores are filled

A chameleon's brilliant coloring can change in a matter of seconds, thanks to pigment-containing cells in the animal's skin.

with pigments of various colors. Changes in the color of the skin occur when signals from the animal's nervous system shrink or stretch certain chromatophores.

Body Language

Raising a feathery crest or changing color is a visual display—a message meant to be seen. Display is commonly used for courtship, to threaten, and to send an alarm. Many displays use body language, such as facial expressions, movements, and postures (ways of standing).

An animal's body language sometimes looks familiar to humans, but animals and humans may use the same body language to send very different messages. If a baboon or a hippopotamus opens its mouth wide and yawns, for example, it might be a good idea to get out of its way. A big yawn does not mean that the animal is tired or bored—showing its teeth is a sign of aggression.

The yawn of a hippopotamus communicates aggression, not sleepiness. Although hippos are plant eaters, they have massive, sharp teeth for fighting and self-defense.

Amphibians: Newt Acrobatics

The desire to find a mate can make animals do all kinds of things. Great crested newts are pond-dwelling amphibians that live in Europe. The males of this species perform acrobatic visual displays to impress females. They do handstands on their front feet while waving their tails in the air. The male newt is not clowning around, though. All that tail waving also blows his sex pheromones toward the female.

Birds: Courtship Dances

Many birds perform courtship dances. Male and female blue-footed boobies, which live in the Galápagos Islands and other Pacific islands, dance with each other. Waddling from side to side, they slowly raise their bright blue feet to display them to each other and then rub their necks and beaks together to cement their bond.

A male and a female blue-footed booby, birds native to islands in the Pacific Ocean, perform a slow, solemn dance together during their courtship.

43

Often males dance to impress females, who simply stand and watch the show. The male peafowl, called a peacock, is famous for his train—his gorgeous tail of long, shining blue-green feathers with eyespots at the end. The fanning of the tail is the main element of the peacock's courtship dance.

When a peahen is near, the peacock raises his train but turns his back so that she sees the brown underside of the feathers, not their colorful upper surfaces. He steps closer to her. Then, if she does not move away, he turns to display the brilliant colors and eyespots of his train. He may even drop the train on top of her. The peahen either accepts him as her mate or moves on to look for a more appealing peacock.

Mammals: Who's the Boss?

Wolves live in packs, and their body language sends messages about their status in the group. The top-ranking, or dominant, animals, sometimes called the alpha male and alpha female, stand tall, with tail and ears raised. Lower-ranking wolves crouch in submissive or obedient postures. A submissive wolf tucks its tail beneath its body and lowers its ears to show that it recognizes the alpha wolves' superior rank. Depending on an individual wolf's status in the pack, he or she may be submissive to some wolves but dominant over others. Similar behavior is seen in other social mammals, including chimpanzees and coyotes.

The peacock's tail is one of the most splendid visual signals in the animal world. The peahen, the female of the species, is drab by comparison and lacks a fancy tail—but she is the one who decides whether or not to mate.

DO SQUID HAVE A SECRET LANGUAGE?

Squid, octopuses, and cuttlefish are undersea artists. These big-headed, many-armed creatures, called cephalopods, have chromatophores in their skin. By manipulating these cells, the cephalopod switches colors and patterns almost instantly.

Cephalopods use camouflage. They change their appearance to blend into a background of sand, rock, or coral. A change in appearance may also send a message. A resting cuttlefish turns bright yellow to scare away a fish that might eat it. A squid sends ripples of bright colors across its body as a courtship signal to possible mates.

The problem with easy-to-see messages is that predators can see them, too. The sender of the message becomes an easy target. Scientists now think that cephalopods may be able to camouflage themselves for protection and communicate with other cephalopods at the same time. The secret is their double layer of skin cells.

Beneath a cephalopod's chromatophore skin layer is another layer with cells called iridophores. The iridophores reflect light that is polarized (waves of polarized light vibrate in a slightly different way from normal light).

Sharks and other predators cannot see polarized light, but other cephalopods can. The ability to see polarized light is called P-vision. In 2009 researchers suggested that cephalopods may communicate with each other by using polarized light. A squid, for example, could camouflage itself from sharks with its chromatophore skin layer while its iridophore layer sends a "hello, there" message to a squid of the opposite sex.

A cuttlefish has turned itself vivid yellow, hoping to scare off a fish that might eat it. When resting, though, the cuttlefish becomes a mottled gray-brown that blends into its background.

The Sounds of Animal Communication

Movie soundtracks use animal sounds to set a mood. The howl of a wolf or the hoot of an owl can seem eerie, even scary. The chatter of monkeys and parrots plays up the exotic, adventurous feeling of a jungle scene. The trill of birdsong suggests joy. However, these are human interpretations of animal sounds. Those sounds have meanings to animals that scientists do not yet fully understand.

Many animal sounds are **vocalizations**—chirps, calls, howls, or songs—produced by lungs and vocal cords, much as human sounds are produced. Mammals, birds, reptiles, and amphibians all make vocalizations. Some also send sound messages in other ways, such as clicking their teeth, drumming their beak against a tree, or flapping their wings.

Sound travels in waves, and all sounds have frequencies—a measure of the distance between the waves. Low-pitched sounds, such as rumbles and roars, have low frequencies. High-pitched sounds, such as squeaks and screams, have high frequencies. Because low-pitched sounds tend to travel farther than high-pitched ones, animals use low-pitched calls to communicate over distance. Alarm calls, though, do not have to travel far. Many of them are high-pitched.

Insects and Spiders: The Stridulators

Insects, spiders, and fish make sounds by rubbing body parts together. This phenomenon is called **stridulation**. The sounds of grasshoppers and crickets (sometimes called chirps) are stridulations made when the insects scrape their legs against their wings.

The African baboon spider and other members of the tarantula family are sometimes called "hissing spiders" because of the sounds they make, but those sounds are not true hisses. The spiders create the sound by rubbing the stiff hairs on their front legs together. Ants stridulate, too. When an ant rubs its waist against its abdomen, it produces a high-pitched, squeaky sound.

When threatened, South African baboon spiders raise their front legs and show their fangs. The sound they make by rubbing their stiff hairs together has earned them the nickname "hissing spiders."

49

Birds: Squawks and Songs

Bird sounds are among the best-studied vocalizations in the animal kingdom. The songs and calls of birds are so distinctive that an experienced bird-watcher can identify many species just by hearing their vocalizations.

Most birds have a vocabulary of sounds for different occasions. Parents and chicks recognize each other by contact calls that they can hear even in the midst of other noisy birds—in a colony of king penguins, for example. Birds make alarm calls when they sense danger or are attacked and territorial calls to defend their feeding or breeding sites. During mating season, males make courtship calls to attract females. Both males and females may make soft cooing or gurgling calls during courtship or when rearing their young.

The most elaborate calls come from a group of birds called songbirds. While other birds will croak, grunt, whistle, squawk, and click, the songbirds produce musical-sounding notes, which are sometimes strung together into long phrases.

Black-capped chickadees, small North American songbirds, often act as lookouts for whole communities of birds. When a chickadee spots a hawk, owl, or other predatory bird perched on a branch, it gives a type of alarm called a mobbing call. The call signals other small birds in the area to "mob," or harass, the predator. They do so by crowding around the predator while flapping their wings and making noise. There is some risk that the predator will snatch one of the mobbing birds, but mobbing usually makes the predator leave the area, a huge relief to all the mobbers.

Scientists have known since the 1990s that other songbird species recognize the mobbing call of the black-capped chickadee. In 2005, though, researchers discovered that by changing the length or pattern of the call, the chickadee gives other chickadees more details about the threat. A chickadee's call to harass a great horned owl high in a pine, for example, differs from the same chickadee's call to mob a small pygmy owl on a low branch. (The pygmy owl is more dangerous to chickadees and other little birds because it is able to maneuver easily and can pursue its prey into thickets.)

The same researchers then studied red-breasted nuthatches, songbirds that often feed near chickadees. The nuthatches appeared to know the meanings of the specific chickadee calls that they overheard. Like the chickadees, the nuthatches understood the difference in the calls to mob the great horned owl and the pygmy owl. Birds, it seems, are not just good communicators—some of them are also good eavesdroppers.

Sea Mammals: Mysterious Songs

Dolphins, porpoises, and whales are sea mammals, members of an aquatic order called cetaceans. For cetaceans, sound is an excellent way to communicate. Sound waves travel more quickly through water than through air, and sound travels much farther through water than light does.

Most cetacean species communicate by whistling, clicking, and forcing air through a cavity in the head and out through the blowhole to make chattering or squealing sounds. A species called the bottle-nosed dolphin communicates by means of whistles. Some researchers claim to have identified hundreds of different types of whistles. In addition, each individual dolphin's signature whistle is distinct and recognizable. Belugas, which are white Arctic whales, have an even larger vocabulary of chirps, squeaks, and whistles. Because these sounds reminded sailors of the singing birds called canaries, belugas gained the nickname "sea canaries."

Baleen whales are cetaceans that make sounds without using their blowholes. Scientists are not yet sure how these whales do it. Air may move around inside the whale's body and create sound waves that pass through it into the water.

The baleen whales' sounds include high-frequency chirps and whistles and low-frequency grunts, moans, and knocks. The low-frequency sounds travel through the water for distances up to hundreds of miles (1 mile = 1.6 km). In addition, some baleen species, such as the blue whale and the humpback whale, produce long series of repeated sound patterns that have been called "songs."

Whale songs may last for half an hour, and a whale may repeat one pattern for days at a time. It has been found that whales in a geographic region sing the same song, which is different from the song of the same species in other regions. For example, blue whales that live near Japan sing one song, those near Chile sing a different song, and those in Antarctic waters sing a third song. As the song changes slowly over time, each whale in the region learns the new version.

Thousands of hours of whale songs have been recorded, but scientists do not yet know what the songs mean or why whales produce them. Some zoologists are not convinced that whales use the songs to communicate with each other. Most researchers, though, think that the songs are a kind of communication that may be related to courtship.

Land Mammals: Coyotes, Monkeys, and More

Coyotes make a lot of noise at night. When they are foraging alone, they keep in touch with other pack members through two vocalizations; howling and barking. Howls are long and usually contain high-pitched yelping sounds followed by wails. Barks are shorter and higher-pitched. Howls seem to carry information about what the coyotes are doing, such as protecting pups or finding food. Barks help the animals judge their distance and direction from each other.

Scientists are learning that many animal sounds are full of previously unsuspected information. For example, the loud, wild-sounding vocalizations of the spotted hyena were called laughter or giggling, but no one knew what they meant until 2009, when researchers recorded and studied hundreds of hours of sounds made by twenty-six hyenas. Vocalizations were classified by the hyenas that made them and the circumstances in which each sound was made, such as greeting another hyena or fighting over food. Using computers to analyze the sounds, the researchers uncovered layers of meaning in the famous giggles.

The pitch of a giggle reveals the hyena's age. The arrangement of notes matches the animal's rank in the clan. Giggling seems to help hyenas keep the social order sorted out when the clan gathers around a carcass, with each member trying to snatch bites.

Primate sounds have been well studied because humans are primates, and the communications of monkeys and apes may hold clues to the origins of human language. Monkeys and apes cannot form the words of human languages—their throats and mouths are too different from humans'. Some experts, however, think that apes can communicate with humans in other ways, such as through sign language. While animal intelligence researchers investigate that question, other scientists study how wild monkeys and apes communicate with each other.

In 1980 primatologists examined the alarm calls of vervet monkeys, small African primates. To their surprise, the researchers discovered that the monkeys had different alarms for various dangers. One call meant "snake." Vervets that heard that call looked down at the ground. The "eagle" call made them look up at the sky. With the "leopard" call the vervets climbed high in the trees. It was the first time that such a complex vocabulary was identified in a monkey species.

Since then scientists have found that other monkeys use different alarm calls for different kinds of predators. (So do some other animals, including mongooses, prairie dogs—and, of course, black-capped chickadees.) Still, in the first decade of the twenty-first century, scientists were astonished to learn that monkeys may have grammar, which is a way of stringing together the building blocks of language in combinations that create meaning.

Researchers in West Africa studied the calls of Campbell's monkeys, primates that live in groups of eight to a dozen animals in

Vervet monkeys warn others in their troop against danger by using a special call for each type of predator, such as an eagle, snake, or leopard.

African forests. The researchers found that this species of monkey has six basic calls, including *boom-boom* ("here I am" or "come here"), *krak!* ("leopard alert!"), and *hok!* ("eagle alert!"). According to the researchers, however, the meaning changes when monkeys combine these calls or add the sound *-oo*. *Krak-oo*, for example, seems to mean "predator," not "leopard" in particular. *Boom-boom krak-oo krak-oo krak-oo* does not mean "come here" *or* "predator." It means "Watch out! Falling tree!"

Much more research is needed before scientists agree on this interpretation of the monkeys' calls. If it proves to be true, however, it will be an important breakthrough in the study of animal communication. It will mean that Campbell's monkeys have not just a language but also a kind of grammar.

Chimpanzees are of special interest to primate researchers because they are humans' closest nonhuman relatives. After years of observing wild chimpanzees, scientists know that these animals have a vocabulary of about three dozen separate sounds, made up of barks, hoots, pants, grunts, and screams. They communicate for many purposes—to signal their location, warn of a prowling leopard, challenge a dominant member of the troop, make peace after a spat, and soothe an infant. Chimps say *Hoo, hoo, hoo* to stay in contact with each other, for example, and *Waaa!* (a barking sound) while watching other chimps fight.

There is a big difference between human and chimpanzee communication. Chimps send messages to communicate information, but they do not have back and forth conversations, as humans do.

Messages Humans Can't Hear

Some animals communicate with sounds humans cannot hear. Sound pitched so high that the human ear cannot detect it is called ultrasound. Sound below the range of human hearing is known as infrasound.

Ultrasound Messages

Scientists have known for a long time that cats, dolphins, bats, and some other animals hear ultrasound. That is why dogs can hear "silent" dog whistles. These whistles produce ultrasound. The dog can hear it, but the person blowing the whistle doesn't hear a thing.

In 2010 scientists reported that ordinary house mice use ultrasound for courtship. After smelling the pheromones of female mice, male mice sang songs in the ultrasound range. The songs varied in length and arrangement. No one yet knows what makes a mouse's song a hit, but females preferred songs sung by males that were not related to them. The songs may help mice tell the difference between family members and strangers so that they can choose strangers as mates to avoid inbreeding.

Infrasound Messages

In the 1980s scientists working at an Oregon zoo discovered why elephants sometimes perk up their ears, even though humans in the same area cannot hear anything. The elephants are hearing messages from other elephants. These huge mammals, it turns out, communicate with low-pitched infrasound.

The okapi, a relative of the giraffe, is one of several animals that communicate using infrasound, vibrations too low-pitched for human ears. Infrasound travels a long way, making it a good communication medium for animals that occupy large territories in dense rain forest.

Elephant calls span a wide range of frequencies. Humans can hear elephants' trumpeting calls, but they do not hear the part of the call that sinks into the infrasound range—although some researchers claim to feel a rumbling sensation like "silent thunder" when elephants vocalize in the infrasound range.

Because of its low frequencies, infrasound travels a long way, making it useful for animals that roam large territories. During the 1990s zoologists found that infrasound communication is used by alligators, hippopotamuses, rhinoceroses, giraffes, and okapi (relatives of giraffes). The search is on for more examples of animal infrasound.

4. FEELING IT

Not all animal messages are smelled, tasted, seen, or heard. Some are felt. When a chimpanzee grooms another chimp's fur or a lonely male alligator thrashes his tail in the water or a deathwatch beetle bangs its head against a piece of wood, the animal is sending a message that other animals will feel. From elephants to honeybees, thousands of species communicate by touch and vibration.

Up Close and Personal

Touch is the most direct form of communication, although it works only over short distances—as far as an animal can reach. A lot of communication that is **tactile** (that is, based on touch) is related to bonding and social ties. Sometimes, though, it involves hostility, as when two animals fight over territory or a mate.

Touch is a big part of courtship for many animals. In some fish species, the female signals that she is ready for mating by biting the

Chimpanzees and other primates spend a lot of time grooming each other. Grooming cleans their fur and removes parasites, but it is also an important kind of communication that reinforces ties among family and troop members.

side of a male. Alligators rub snouts. Giraffes twine their long necks together. Elephants do the same thing with their trunks. Male and female lions rub their sides together and lick each other's face during courtship—an action that may communicate two ways, through touch and through chemicals from the scent glands on the lion's cheeks. All of these actions are messages that build a pair bond.

Insects: Follow the Leader

Social insects do much of their communicating with pheromones, but some use touch, too. Shore ants, which live along western European seacoasts, make scent trails to lead other ants to newly discovered food. Other ants do the same thing, but the shore ant adds tactile communication to the message. When the finder ant returns to the food, a recruit ant runs right behind it and taps constantly on the finder's body with its antennae to signal that it is following. If the tapping stops, the finder slows down and waits for the recruit to catch up.

Birds: Cleaning and Preening

Courting birds preen each other's feathers (preening is the cleaning and straightening of the feathers with the beak). Young birds learn to preen by imitating their parents, who preen the young to reinforce the bond between parents and offspring. At a certain point, though, the parents may stop preening the young. It is their way of saying, "It's time for you to leave the nest and head out into the world on your own."

Mammals: Building a Bond

Mammals often lick their newborn young, not just to clean them but also to cover them with pheromones that the young animals will recognize. Mother elephants and their young frequently caress each other with their trunks. If a young elephant needs discipline, the mother will also use the trunk to slap it.

Touch is important for animals that spend their whole lives in family or social groups. Elephants live in small family herds made up of adult females and young elephants of both sexes. (Adult males live on their own and join the females only for mating.) Within these herds, the elephants stay physically close to one another. They often stand with their sides touching while eating or resting.

Chimpanzees make much use of a particular kind of tactile communication known as grooming. They pick through each other's fur and remove insects, dirt, and bits of vegetation. Young chimps learn to groom from their mother.

As adults, chimps groom in all kinds of social arrangements. Mating pairs groom each other. So do siblings and pairs of friends. Groups groom together to strengthen their social bonds or to make peace after an argument. Low-ranking chimps groom high-ranking chimps to get on the big shot's good side. Sometimes, to gain allies and support in a power struggle, high-ranking chimps turn the tables and groom low-ranking ones. Time spent sitting in pairs or groups, linked by touch, is an important part of chimpanzee communication.

SHOCKING SIGNALS

Electric signals travel through all animals, including humans, and create a field of electricity around the body. These fields are so faint that only fish and a few other animals can sense them.

Fish "read" electrical fields with special organs called electroreceptors, arranged in lines on their sides. The electroreceptors pick up electrical signals, which travel well through water. Many fish find prey by tracking their electrical fields. For a few fish—electric eels and rays—electricity is a weapon. They can give off electrical discharges strong enough to stun their prey.

Only two groups of fish are known to communicate with electricity. African freshwater elephantfish send electrical messages when fighting. Their electrical fields become stronger as conflict approaches. When the fish attack each other with agonistic moves, such as head butting, their electrical signals change. The South American knifefish, meanwhile, use electrical signals for courtship, not hostility. Males and females of each knifefish species have signals unique to each sex that help them find each other in murky river water. At mating time the female lays her eggs when the male changes the frequency of his signal. There may be many more examples of animal electrocommunication not yet known to science.

In water that is too murky or weedy for clear vision, South American knifefish rely on electric signals to find mates.

Getting a Vibe

If you have ever felt the floor shake a little when someone slammed a door or stamped a foot, you have experienced vibratory communication. Many animals send messages in the form of vibrations that travel through the air, water, or ground.

Spiders and Insects: The Quest for a Mate

Vibrations travel easily along the fine silk strands of a spiderweb. When an orb-weaver spider feels its web vibrating, it knows that a fly or some other prey, struggling and thrashing, is trapped in the sticky web. The vibrations are like a dinner bell, and the spider runs out to make a meal of the prey.

Sometimes, though, the male spider vibrates a web to court a female. Because female spiders are likely to regard a male of their own species as prey except at mating time, the male orb-weaver sends a mating message. The male taps on a female's web with its jaw and

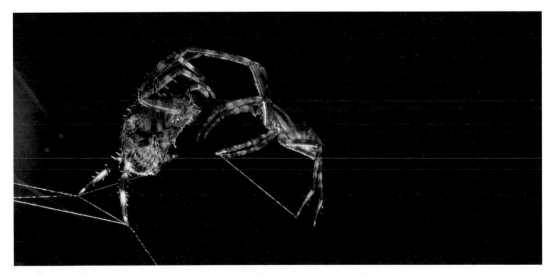

A male cross spider (*right*) has made a cautious approach to a heavier, stronger female. If he has sent the right signals, he will mate with her. If there was a glitch in their communication, though, she will eat him.

abdomen using a special mating signal that the female instinctively recognizes. The ritual works for the male most of the time. Sometimes, though, a female misses or ignores the message and eats the unlucky male.

Green stinkbug beetles combine smell and vibration to communicate with possible mates. The male sends out a cloud of pheromones, and a nearby female looking for a mate smells the pheromones and flies toward the male. Airborne smells do not always lead a female to the male's precise location, however. If she gets close but cannot find him, she lands on a plant and vibrates her abdomen against it. She sends out a series of bursts, waits five seconds, and repeats the pattern. The male stinkbug senses her vibrations through his feet. He moves around until he feels the vibrations getting stronger in a particular direction, and then he follows the "vibration trail" to the female. Along the way he sends his own vibrations to tell her that he is on his way.

The deathwatch beetle, which lives in trees and wooden structures, has a hard head and sensitive feet. A male finds a female (or the other way around) by tapping its head against wood. Each listens for the other's message; they move closer together after each one. Although people may hear the beetles' knocks, the beetles sense the taps as vibrations in the pads on their feet.

Reptiles: Murky Waters

For alligators and other animals that live in dark or muddy water, vibration is a good way to communicate. Alligators have a good sense of

An alligator's deep roar or bellow travels far over the water of a swamp or lake. These reptiles also send out messages through infrasound and vibrations in the water.

smell, but they are also very good at picking up vibratory signals. An alligator's face and jaws are covered with small sense organs called dome pressure receptors. These receptors react to pressure waves in the water. Some pressure waves are created by prey such as fish and turtles, but some waves are messages from other alligators.

The male alligator, called a bull, sends signals through the water by slapping its head on the surface and swinging its powerful tail from side to side. Alligators also create vibrations when they bellow. The bellow starts as a deep infrasound vibration that shakes the water, sometimes strongly enough to throw droplets into the air. Then the bellow rises in pitch and becomes a sound that humans can hear. A bull alligator bellows to mark its territory. As part of courtship, the male and female bellow at each other.

Mammals: Talking with Feet and Trunks

Creatures large and small communicate by means of seismic waves, which are vibrations that travel through the ground. The banner-tailed kangaroo rat of the American Southwest is one of several rodents that thump out messages—and receive them—with their large rear feet.

Every kangaroo rat has its own pattern of thumps, a form of vibrational identification that other rats recognize. When a rat picks up a seismic signal from a family or community member, it answers with its own signal. It is the kangaroo rat's way of saying, "It's me." A stronger vibratory signal warns intruders away from the rat's territory.

Elephants, too, have nerves in their feet that are sensitive to the pressure of seismic waves. These nerves are also found near the end of an elephant's trunk. An elephant can pick up ground vibrations through its feet and through its trunk when the trunk is resting on the ground.

In this way an elephant senses seismic vibrations from other elephants' infrasound calls. These vibrations travel through the ground for many miles, much farther than they could be heard as **auditory** signals. Elephants also create seismic signals by stamping their feet. As they roam a large territory, elephants use these long-distance messages to keep in touch with other herds, to locate mates, and to send alarm calls.

Decoding the Dance of the Bees

The Austrian biologist Karl von Frisch made the discovery that bees communicate using a dance language. Although von Frisch announced this discovery in 1923, it did not become widely known until the 1960s, when his research was published in English.

A honeybee sometimes "dances" inside a bees' nest; the dance consists of the bee waggling its body from side to side as it traces a pattern on the wall of the honeycomb. Before von Frisch, no one understood this behavior, but he claimed to have figured it out. The "waggle dance" of the honeybee, von Frisch said, was a complex form of communication.

The Language of Dance

The dancing bee, von Frisch explained, is a scout that has just discovered a new source of nectar, such as a patch of flowers, some distance from the nest. The dance is the scout's way of telling other bees where to find the food. Two vital pieces of information—the direction of the food from the nest and the distance to the food—are communicated by different parts of the dance.

The dance starts when the scout runs in a straight line on the honeycomb wall while waggling its abdomen from side to side and vibrating its wings. At the end of the run, the scout turns to one

A diagram illustrates the honeybee's waggle dance. A scout bee tells of a food source during the "straight run" part of the dance, the vertical line up the center of the figure eight. Nearby bees sense the scout's movements, which tell them the distance and direction of the food.

side, runs in a half circle back to the beginning, and then runs along the line again. This time the scout turns in the other direction and makes another half circle back to the beginning of the line. The result is a pattern like a squashed figure eight. The scout repeats the dance until other bees start flying to the food source.

The important part of the dance is the straight line in the middle, which is where the messages appear. The time the bee spends running in the straight line communicates the distance to the food. If the bee's straight run lasts for 2.5 seconds, for example, the food is about 8,600 feet (2,625 meters [m]) away—more than a mile and a half. The waggling abdomen and beating wings also communicate information about distance. Slow waggles and long buzzes mean longer distances. Rapid waggles and short, quick buzzes mean shorter distances.

The angle of the dance communicates the direction to the food relative to the position of the sun outside the nest. If the bee runs straight up the wall, the food is in the same direction as the sun. If the bee runs straight down the wall, the food is exactly opposite the sun's position. If the bee runs up at a 45-degree angle, the direction to the food is 45 degrees away from the sun's position.

Robot Bees and Tiny Breezes

Even though von Frisch shared a 1973 Nobel Prize for decoding the dance of the honeybees, some scientists still questioned whether he was right about the dance. They thought bees learned about the new food source from flower odors on the scout's body, not from the dance. They also wondered how the bees could sense the scout's movements in the dark nest.

Decades of research have shown that both von Frisch and his critics were right. The waggle dance does tell bees about the location of a food source, but not with pinpoint accuracy. Some bees recruited by a dance never find the food or find it only after several tries. Many bees reach the right general area but must then fly around for a while before they track down the food by sight and smell.

To test von Frisch's ideas, scientists started in the late 1980s to build tiny robot bees that could perform the waggle dance. The first robot bees were large and clunky compared with the newest models, which can be programmed to imitate variations in the dance. These tools have helped scientists understand how scout bees communicate using dance *and* scent.

If scientists put no flower odors on a robot bee before it dances, the recruited bees do not find the food. Many do not even bother to look

The honeybee on the left senses the vibrations of a robot bee controlled by researchers. If the real bee finds the food source after receiving the robot's message, the researchers will know that they succeeded in "talking" to a bee in its own language.

for it. Without scent, the dance is not enough. However, when scientists put flower scent on the robot, the other bees watch the dance and then set out to find the food, and most of them succeed. In 2005, after using radar to track the flights of recruited bees, researchers reported that the combination of dance and flower scents led bees to within 5 yards (4.5 m) of a food source 200 yards (182 m) from the nest.

Even the mystery of how bees see the scout's dance has been solved thanks to miniature sensors invented for use in manufacturing computer chips. These sensors can measure the tiniest movements of air. In 2007 scientists reported on a study of bee communication using the sensors to record air flow in bees' nests during the waggle dance. They found that the scout's movement creates small jets of air, as well as sound waves. Other bees sense these jets and waves through organs in their antennae, body hairs, and membranes that react to pressure and vibration. The bees sense the scout's movements by the angle of the air jets and the sound waves. Bees do not see the waggle dance at all—they just feel it.

The dance of the honeybees is one of the most complex communications in nature. Nearly a century after the dance was discovered, scientists are still learning about it, and they have learned about many other remarkable kinds of animal communication as well. The sight of a bee flying on its way to a flower is a small reminder that the world is full of creatures exchanging messages. The exploration of the marvels of animal communication has just begun.

GLOSSARY

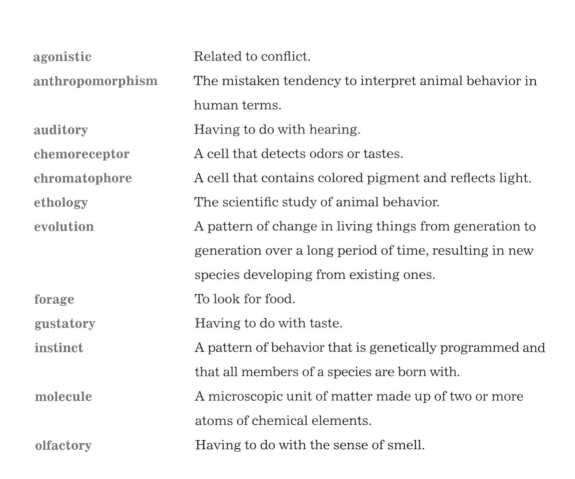

agonistic	Related to conflict.
anthropomorphism	The mistaken tendency to interpret animal behavior in human terms.
auditory	Having to do with hearing.
chemoreceptor	A cell that detects odors or tastes.
chromatophore	A cell that contains colored pigment and reflects light.
ethology	The scientific study of animal behavior.
evolution	A pattern of change in living things from generation to generation over a long period of time, resulting in new species developing from existing ones.
forage	To look for food.
gustatory	Having to do with taste.
instinct	A pattern of behavior that is genetically programmed and that all members of a species are born with.
molecule	A microscopic unit of matter made up of two or more atoms of chemical elements.
olfactory	Having to do with the sense of smell.

pheromone	A chemical given off by an animal that causes a behavioral response in other animals of the same species.
predator	An animal that preys on or hunts and eats other animals.
prey	An animal that is hunted or killed by a predator.
primate	One of a group of animals that includes monkeys, apes, and humans.
primatologist	One who studies primates.
psychology	The scientific study of mental and behavioral characteristics; comparative psychologists study the differences and similarities between human and animal minds.
sociobiologist	A scientist who studies how animals that live in social groups, such as ants and zebras, interact with each other.
species	A group of plants or animals that are similar enough to produce fertile offspring (that is, offspring able to produce offspring of their own).
stridulation	A squeaking or chirping sound that insects or spiders make by rubbing body parts (such as legs) together.
tactile	Related to touch.
vocalization	A sound made by passing air from the lungs over the vocal cords.
vomeronasal organ	A patch of special skin in the roof of the mouth of some animals that senses pheromones and other molecules in the air; also called Jacobson's organ.
zoology	A branch of biology that studies animals, including insects.

FIND OUT MORE

Books

Chinery, Michael. *How Animals Communicate*. London: Southwater, 2005.

Ganeri, Anita. *Animal Communication*. New York: Chelsea House, 2004.

Kalman, Bobbie. *How Do Animals Communicate?* New York: Crabtree Publishing Company, 2009.

Tatham, Betty. *How Animals Communicate*. New York: Franklin Watts, 2004.

Tomecek, Stephen M. *Animal Communication*. New York: Chelsea House, 2009.

Websites

All about Birds

www.allaboutbirds.org/NetCommunity/Page.aspx?pid=1189

All about Birds, part of the Cornell Lab of Ornithology site, has photographs, video, and sound recordings of hundreds of species of birds.

Animal Communication Project

http://acp.eugraph.com/

Stephen Hart, a biologist and journalist and the author of *The Language of Animals*, presents research into communication among many types of animals. Included are links to articles on other sites.

Dances with Bees

www.pbs.org/wgbh/nova/bees/dances.html

NOVA Online's site about bee dances has interactive videos of bees performing a variety of communication dances.

Kay Holekamp Laboratory: Behavioral Ecology and Evolution

http://hyenas.zoology.msu.edu/

The website of animal researcher Kay Holekamp, who teaches at Michigan State University and studies hyenas in Africa, features blog entries and a video about her work with spotted hyenas on the Masai Mara reserve in Kenya, including investigations of hyena communication.

The Whalesong Project

www.whalesong.net/

Songs of humpback whales from Hawaiian waters.

BIBLIOGRAPHY

The author found these books and articles especially helpful.

Amé, Jean-Marc, et al. "Collegial Decision Making Based on Social Amplification Leads to Optimal Group Formation." *Proceedings of the National Academy of Sciences*, April 11, 2006, vol. 103, no. 15: 5835–5840.

Anderson, Stephen R. *Doctor Doolittle's Delusion: Animals and the Uniqueness of Human Language*. New Haven, CT: Yale University Press, 2004.

Brockmann, Axel, and Gene E. Robinson. "Central Projections of Sensory Systems Involved in Honey Bee Dance Language Communication." *Brain, Behavior, and Evolution*, 2007, no. 70: 125–136, www.life.illinois.edu/robinson/Research/Pdf/ Looking for the Dance Language Center in the Bee Brain.pdf

Burkhardt, Richard W. Jr. *Patterns of Behavior: Konrad Lorenz, Niko Tinbergen, and the Founding of Ethology*. Chicago: University of Chicago Press, 2005.

Clayton, David. "Singing and Dancing in the Ghost Crab *Ocypode platytarsus*." *Journal of Natural History* 42, nos. 3–4 (January 2008): 141–155.

de Waal, Frans. *The Ape and the Sushi Master: Cultural Reflections of a Primatologist*. New York: Basic Books, 2001.

Dudzinski, Kathleen. *Dolphin Mysteries: Unlocking the Secrets of Communication*. New Haven, CT: Yale University Press, 2008.

Flores, Graciela. "Squid Secrets." *Natural History* 116, no. 1 (February 2007): 15.

Hart, Stephen. *The Language of Animals*. 2nd ed. New York: Henry Holt, 1996.

Hauser, Marc D. *The Design of Animal Communication*. Cambridge, MA: MIT Press, 2003.

Hill, Peggy S. M. *Vibrational Communication in Animals*. Cambridge, MA: Harvard University Press, 2008.

Kessler, Rebecca. "Animal Party Line." *Natural History* 117, no. 8 (October 2008): 16.

Manning, Aubrey, and Marian Stamp Dawkins. *Animal Behavior*. 5th ed. Cambridge, UK: Cambridge University Press, 1998.

McGregor, Peter K. *Animal Communication Networks*. Cambridge, UK: Cambridge University Press, 2005.

Michelsen, Axel. "Signals and Flexibility in the Dance Communication of Honeybees." *Journal of Comparative Physiology* 189, no. 3 (March 2003): 165–174.

Milius, Susan. "Myth of the Bad-Nose Birds: Study of Avian Sense of Smell Recovers from Audubon's Blunder." *Science News*, August 20, 2005, findarticles. com/p/articles/mi_m1200/is_8_168/ai_n15393211/

O'Connell, Caitlin. *The Elephant's Secret Sense: The Hidden Life of the Wild Herds of Africa*. Chicago: University of Chicago Press, 2007.

Riley, J. R., et al. "The Flight Paths of Honeybees Recruited by the Waggle Dance." *Nature* 435 (May 12, 2005): 205–207.

Rogers, Lesley J. *Songs, Roars, and Rituals: Communication in Birds, Mammals, and Other Animals*. Cambridge, MA: Harvard University Press, 2000.

Searcy, William A., and Stephen Nowicki. *The Evolution of Animal Communication: Reliability and Deception in Signalling Systems*. Princeton, NJ: Princeton University Press, 2005.

Skov, Charlotte, and Jim Wiley. "Establishment of the Neotropical Orchid Bee *Euglossa Viridissima* (Hymenoptera: Apidae) in Florida." *Florida Entomologist* 88, no. 2 (June 2005): 225–227, www.fcla.edu/FlaEnt/fe88p225.pdf

Slobodchikoff, C. N. *Prairie Dogs: Communication and Community in an Animal Society*. Cambridge, MA: Harvard University Press, 2009.

Smith, John Maynard, and David Harper. *Animal Signals*. New York: Oxford University Press, 2003.

Tarpy, David R. "The Honeybee Dance Language." North Carolina Cooperative Extension Service, April 2004, www.cals.ncsu.edu/entomology/apiculture/PDF%20files/1.11.pdf

Templeton, Christopher N., and Erick Greene. "Nuthatches eavesdrop on variations in heterospecific chickadee mobbing alarm calls." *Proceedings of the National Academy of Science* 104, no. 13 (March 27, 2007): 5479–5482.

Uhlenbroek, Charlotte, ed. *Animal Life*. New York: Dorling Kindersley, 2008.

Viegas, Jennifer. "Male Mice Sing Ultrasonic Love Songs."*Discovery News*. March 5, 2010, http://news.discovery.com/animals/mouse-courtship-songs-ultrasonic.html

Wade, Nicholas. "Deciphering the Chatter of Monkeys and Chimps." *New York Times*, January 11, 2010, www.nytimes.com/2010/01/12/science/12monkey.html?_r=1&sq=vervet%20monkey%20communication&st=cse&scp=3&pagewanted=all.

———. "Boom! Hok! A Monkey Language Is Deciphered." *New York Times*, December 7, 2009, www.nytimes.com/2009/12/08/science/08monkey.html?sq=vervet%20monkey%20communication&st=cse&adxnnl=1&scp=1&adxnnlx=1279753252-D2ZQ+QwCuGISnjr5tlKSkw

Wyatt, Tristram D. *Pheromones and Animal Behavior: Communication by Smell and Taste*. Cambridge, UK: Cambridge University Press, 2003.

INDEX

REBECCA STEFOFF has written many books about animals for young readers of all ages. Her book *Ant* (1998) was made into a chapter in a popular reading textbook for second graders. Since then Stefoff has written ten books, including *Horses*, *Penguins*, *Chimpanzees*, and *Tigers*, in the AnimalWays series for young adults. For the same publisher's Family Trees series, she explored twelve groups of living things, from *The Fungus Kingdom* to *The Primate Order*. Stefoff lives in Portland, Oregon, where she enjoys bird-watching, kayaking, and visiting the zoo. You can learn more about her and her books for young people at www.rebeccastefoff.com.